39 Ways of Looking

By the same author:

Poetry

Seventy-Seven Poems
The Angel and the Fox
Approaching Animals from A to Z

Biography

Louis Jennings MP,
Editor of the *New York Times* and Tory Democrat

Born in Huddersfield, David Morphet read English at Cambridge, where he was co-editor of the literary magazine *Delta*. He has worked in the British Diplomatic Service, and has represented the United Kingdom on various international energy bodies. Married, with three grown-up children, he lives in London.

39 Ways of Looking

David Morphet

First published in 2005 by

Notion Books
11 Daisy Lane
London
SW6 3DD
www.notionbooks.co.uk

ISBN 0 9541573 4 6

Designed and produced by
The Short Run Book Company Limited
Unit 1, Orpheus House
Calleva Park
Aldermaston
Berkshire
RG7 4QW

Contents

39 Ways of Looking

i.	Out of Focus	9
ii.	Wheel of Life	10
iii.	Quarter Dollar	11
iv.	Chariot of Fire	12
v.	Deliverance	13
vi.	Rain in Iceland	14
vii.	Rain in the Allgäu	15
viii.	Rain at Innisfree	16
ix.	Winter by Avon	17
x.	Winter in Lebanon	18
xi.	Puncture at Gethsemane	19
xii.	Magi	20
xiii.	Relics	21
xiv.	Luther at the Wartburg	22
xv.	Refugees	23
xvi.	The Angel of Güstrow	24
xvii.	Primo Levi's Chemistry	25
xviii.	Galileo	26
xix.	Lorca at Granada	27
xx.	The Power of Counterpoint	28
xxi.	The Sleep of Reason	29
xxii.	Gauguin's Vision	30
xxiii.	Vincent's Chair	31
xxiv.	Magritte's Mirror	32
xxv.	The Angel of the North	33
xxvi.	The *David* of Michelangelo	34
xxvii.	*Ego Hugo*	35
xxviii.	*Leaves of Grass*	36
xxix.	Shamans	37
xxx.	Oracle	38
xxxi.	Gods at Madurai	39

xxxii.	Pantocrator	40
xxxiii.	Le Thoronet	41
xxxiv.	Candles for the Dead	42
xxxv.	Kyoto Garden	43
xxxvi.	Mandala of Sand	44
xxxvii.	Moore: *Reclining Figure*	45
xxxviii.	Silence at Briggflatts	46
xxxix.	Pen-y-Ghent	47

The Automatic Self

i.	The Automatic Self	49
ii.	Another Man	50
iii.	Heart and Mind	51
iv.	Wound	52
v.	Suppleness	53

Night Watch

i.	Night Watch	55
ii.	The Unreal Estate	59
iii.	Night Flight	60
iv.	Peculiar Readings	61
v.	Time and Again	62

Worlds Apart

i.	Open the Atlas	63
ii.	Mappa Mundi	64
iii.	Golden Age	65
iv.	Surrealist World	66
v.	Peters' Projection	67

Haikus for a Summer Day	68
Haikus for a Winter Day	69
Winter Day above Dent	70
Intrusion	71
Riddle	72

"Our brains ...
are always at work on some quivers
of self-organisation, however faint,
and it is from this that an order
arises ..."

W G Sebald (1944-2001)

[from *After Nature*
tr. Michael Hamburger]

39 Ways of Looking

i.

Out of Focus

Once, half-lost in the sands, I came upon
a Beduin who pointed straightaway
to a far speck of flag I'd failed to see
through glasses trained upon horizon heat
simmering like a molten lake.

In later days I learned to look
with caution at the incumbent view
of how the land lay; or the safest
treads to follow in the sand;
or which unproven track to take

towards an unsure rendezvous.
Some turns can prove a big mistake
and markings complicate a trail
that over years begins to show
that signs are often skew, or fake.

It's still there, the elusive flag –
still far off at the desert's edge
on what I take to be the borders
of a settled land, to which I look
through lenses out of focus and opaque.

ii.

Wheel of Life

Tibetan monks are playing volley-ball
beside a temple in Karnataka.
Since all is known to be illusory,
the game is slow and decorous.
No one will win. There'll be no final score.

The abbot drives us in his four-by-four
around the settlement to show
deep trenches for deterring elephant,
and platforms where the farmers sit at night
with gongs to frighten off wild boar.

Back to the cyber café. Ten rupees
takes us to London via satellite
while monks in saffron and maroon
glance sidelong at their visitors.
Conch and horn boom out through the temple door.

Beyond the stupa, prayer flags convey
petitions on a hundred flapping lines.
We pause beside the Wheel of Life where snake
and cock and boar pursue an endless round
of stealth and rivalry and war.

iii.

Quarter Dollar

In California I stood beneath
a tree of the highest rank of all.
Down among dead leaves and dust I saw
a quarter glint which someone looking up
had fumbled and let fall.

I gave my mind to things of consequence –
the height of the sequoia;
distance of the sun; the speed of light;
and how the universe goes on and on
until there's nothing there at all.

But meanwhile at my feet there lay
an artefact more eloquent
than anything that's yet been trawled
in all their crossings of the sky
by missions from Canaveral.

I leant and picked the quarter up
and pocketed *In God We Trust*,
deciding I'd no time to waste
on thinking of the universe's
endless outward thrust and sprawl .

iv.

Chariot of Fire

Late sunlight firing up the lochs below
our flight-path over Highland glens
was turning water into usquebaugh –
long vats of burning gold upon
the dusky bolster of the moor.

Blake beside me would have lit on
angels in that luminance or seen,
as cockpit caught the setting sun,
Elisha by the aileron,
riding a chariot of fire.

And all for him would be sublime and sure,
and proof against degrees of scorn,
since visionaries know it's more
than tricks of light that turn them on,
and more than any metaphor –

it's the real thing that lies beyond.
He'd see the living waters flow
from lochs which endlessly renew
the spirit's glass. And in the sunlight's flash
he'd see the flight of arrows of desire.

V.

Deliverance

Over the Jebel, close enough to see
our shadow drag a crucifix
across bare scree and precipice,
the starboard engine cut, which left just one
to cover fifty miles of wilderness.

And that began to cough. We made it – just –
in our enfeebled, spluttering Dove
over the Akhdar summits, sharp as glass.
At Muscat's landing strip, a humid air
entered the cabin like deliverance.

Another time, we're flying blind through snow,
ground zero coming up, no runway light.
The pilot rattles off the altitude
and edges down. We listen, knuckles white,
doubting if landing's worth the turbulence.

He falters, hits the throttle hard and soars,
then swings around to have another go
until outvoted in a plebiscite
by those like me who have no wish to die
blind, in a show of confidence.

vi.

Rain in Iceland

Green icefalls melted by torrential rain
gave birth to swollen, glacial streams in flood
across the bare, mile-wide moraine
where we were stuck four days, unfed,
waiting for the storm to bate.

Our guide, phlegmatic, hunkered down
under a porous bivouac
until the Norns arrived or rescue came.
Under the drenching sky we had no choice
but follow suit and sit and wait.

On the fourth night drove up in splosh and muck
a hundred miles from Reykjavik
a huge St Christopher with winch and truck,
who strode into the flood, and brought
a lifeline to us through the spate.

We learned a lesson from that thrust
on purely literary grounds
into the innards of a land
of ice and cloud and emptiness
and sagas painful to relate.

Rain in the Allgäu

Holed up by thunderstorms in Illertal
I peered out from a gasthaus balcony
through sheets of alpine rain towards
a low mist hanging over peaks
capped supposedly with snow

and thought (since landscape is no more
than light diffused) that mountains may
(being by observation changeable
and inconstant) prove
to be only there for show –

a construct of my own mind's eye –
a synthesis of moods (which come and go)
and signals on the retina
snowed under with distortion
and phenomenal overflow –

a flux of data barely worth
all those weary miles of motorway.
A glass of schnappes seemed best and so,
suspending disbelief, I drank and slept
and waited for the hills to glow.

Rain at Innisfree

Rain on the way to Innisfree
told us what we should have known, that dreams
don't bed down with reality.
The bee-loud glade is in the brain –
naïve to think we could transpose

a vision to a daylight duplicate.
Likewise the tower at Ballylee
still showed a chamber arched with stone
but nothing there of poetry.
The swans at Coole belonged to prose.

At Lissadell the blinds were drawn,
no windows open to the south
or silk kimonos to recall
the ageing poet's afterthought.
No souvenir or curio

on offer there or at the Sligo
graveyard, save a tombstone phrase.
And that was all. We failed to find
unfading vestiges of Yeats's dreams,
or capture them on video.

Winter by Avon

By Avon I thought of lilies,
festering, being worse than weeds: the white
turning to brown and then to slime.
A river fog, sharp to the lung,
was spreading slowly through the town.

On gravel paths lay broken sky.
Through sluggish waters grasses trailed.
And by the grey of riverbank
and its reflections' darker grey,
melancholy trees bent down.

Close by, concealed and vigilant
among the fall of Midland murk,
ice hovered at the freezing point.
Soon the day would drop its guard
and let the frost come sliding in.

Not at all like Illyria.
No ducal palace. No Olivia.
No Globe. No Ariel. No Prospero.
No rising Bolingbroke. No Richard sinking
with his hollow crown.

X.

Winter in Lebanon

All seasons here are treacherous.
Cover's in short supply on summer days
when houses under siege run out of shade
and earth is shrivelling and out at sea
there's nothing but a travesty of cloud.

Cover in winter too is niggardly
when the rains do come. At this altitude
the driving wind will pin you down
and snow show footprints as you struggle through
landslips on the mountainside.

Winter will catch you in its sights.
You're under crossfire as the thunder rolls
down from the hills with waterjets.
It's every village for itself.
Each sortie needs a bodyguard.

Best at these times to stay indoors
and keep an eye on no-man's-land
in case the lame soil, drenched and red,
can hold no more and overflows,
turning the terracing to watershed.

xi.

Puncture at Gethsemane

For Kunio K. and Jiro M.

Delay on the Damascus road
meant no Jerusalem till after dark.
And then a puncture – and on Christmas Eve!
We drew up on the ground beside a wall
on which was chalked *Gethsemane*.

Stray pilgrims from the east and west,
we found a refuge for the night
in a strangely providential way –
by virtue of a rusty nail
poked up where Jesus came to pray.

"High up the Mount," they said, "you'll find
a holy house where you may stay."
Panting, we climbed a narrow alley-way
to nuns who nodded when we told our tale,
opened the gate, and bid *entrer*,

and let us share a platter of *cervelles*
they'd buttered for *les pères* who came to dine
in clean soutanes in honour of the day.
Outside was cold and sharp and piercing stars
transfixed the sky of the Nativity.

xii.

Magi

Odds on they came from Babylon,
those wise men following a star,
if "from the East" means "very far"
and "magus" means "astrologer".
We're told the gifts they chose to bring –

gold and frankincense and myrrh –
but not precisely who they were.
And when they saw the infant-king
we do not know what tongue they spoke
or what they said, if anything.

In Matthew's gospel there's no name.
No *Melchior*. No *Balthasar*.
What mattered was the worshipping.
Only much later came the crowns
and camel-trains and colouring.

Without a word, they went away
back east, and by a different road,
avoiding Herod. And that's all.
No way of knowing what they told
the people back in Babylon.

xiii.

Relics

As good as money in the bank,
those bones. They pulled the faithful in
from half of Christendom, who couldn't wait
to shell out silver to the guardians
of sacrum, vertebrae and skull.

And since the holy places knew
supply must satisfy demand,
even a toe with provenance might sell
in markets ripe for miracles
from martyrs' bits, however small,

which, housed in gold, could tender proof
that sanctity is tangible,
that what is holy can be grasped,
and might, with faith, provide a cure
for cankers of the flesh or soul.

And still they lie exhibited in shrines
surrounded by ex-voto body-parts,
those ancient skeletons made reverend,
and eyes of faithful still attend
to holy bones on constant call.

xiv.

Luther at the Wartburg

After the Wall, the shaky Berlin train
to Leipzig for a glimpse of Bach and on
to Eisenach to see the *feste Burg*
where Luther grew his tonsure out
and gave the Testament a German tongue.

Past platform signs for Weimar, Gotha,
places from the past brought back on line,
their baggage shunted from the sidings
to the here and now. Towns blinking,
out of tune, for long unsung.

And to the castle with its own great wall
where Luther, short on compromise
and long on imprecation laid things down
as gospel: Rome was Babylon;
indulgences, the devil's dung.

So many walls around us not yet down.
Fumes hang in the air of *odium
theologicum*, the righteousness
which lights the homicidal gene.
Anathemas we live among.

Refugees

Images of refugees
panic-stricken by the fear
of war and famine and disease,
will insist on coming near,
spoiling my leisure and my ease.

I want to do things just as I please:
tune in to just what I want to hear.
Let governments take proper care of these.
I see no call to interfere
where one has no expertise.

Except that pain begins to squeeze
the mind's inertia into gear.
All that dying by degrees
in time unclogs the deafest ear.
It keeps on till the blindest sees.

But leave aside the journalese
when those images appear.
They don't need words to make the spirit freeze,
those wounds of gun and knife and spear;
the lines of cripples, amputees.

xvi.

The Angel of Güstrow

In memory of Ernst Barlach, sculptor, 1870-1938

Angels should be perpendicular
and bear good tidings, but this bronze
angel juts out like the prow
of a celestial ship; a figurehead
pointing to silence, mute and still.

Arms by his sides, he holds
his revelation tight. His lips are sealed.
Behind their heavy lids, his eyes
are tranced and motionless.
He has no duty to fulfil

except as witness to whom war has killed,
whose names he knows. All rhetoric
would fall to rags before his raked
embodiment of grace
and uplift of angelic will.

No wonder that his countenance fell foul
of demagogues who wanted their
Valhallas wrapped up in a Nazi flag,
paraded through the streets and then
marched with drumming to a future kill.

Primo Levi's Chemistry

No trace of egotistical sublime
contaminates his sombre chemistry.
He keeps his cool, stays rational and calm,
objective and meticulous,
while scoping poisons of the mind,

distilling out iniquities,
describing compounds of the ultra-vile.
He knows that his analysis of what
is darkness and unspeakable may fail
unless precise and well-defined;

and so with utmost pains he filters out
the residues of evil where they lie
in cess and ash and pestilence.
We follow through the Lager gates
into killing-grounds behind,

where as witness he will verify
the death and suffering of those
who sank from sight and drowned in countless shoals,
and for whose fate he catalyses
agonies of heart and mind.

xviii.

Galileo

There comes in superstitious times
a headstrong man who claims the earth
is travelling around the sun,
not vice versa, but a satellite,
subordinate and hanger-on.

But everyone can see the sun
circling daily round the earth.
Say other, and you trouble men
about all centres of authority,
of which Rome is the Number One.

So Galileo has to swerve and tack
under the threat of screw and rack
and state that, after all, the sun
revolves around an earth which is
entirely still, unmoved, unspun.

Poison in the blood and heart,
the bitterness of truth denied.
Poison, though the lie may win,
to those too who stand still and lie,
paralysed by pride and spin.

Lorca at Granada

Where Ferdinand and Isabella lie
under their marble catafalque, I thought
of Lorca in the evil times who knew
how to throw shadows on the face of words
from shadows in the heart.

The one who saw through veil and masquerade
the mottle in the glass, who saw
behind staccato patios
the sterile silences locked up within;
dream and fulfilment far apart.

The town itself a kind of dream,
its ochre walls and palaces
horizoned by the high Nevada snow
and the wide green Granada plain,
sweet water veined through every part.

But beauty spattered with its own red blood.
For its keenest voice and laureate
no catafalque or marble monument
but bullets from a murder squad.
No requiem. *Rat-tat-tat-tat.*

XX.

The Power of Counterpoint

At evening, the flamboyant star who took
the *Fugues and Preludes* from his fingertips
brought Shostakovich to the crowded Hall
like an old friend. It seemed
she brought him close enough to touch,

and in her vigour helped us see
the youthful Nikolayeva
who forty years before played Bach's *Clavier*
in firestormed Leipzig, and inspired
her master to produce another such.

We sat in comfort, free and far removed
from the cold gulag curtain-years
when all of Russia was automaton,
its poets silent and its music ruled
by one who held all keys within his clutch.

Courageous Orpheus to meet
that underworld in counterpoint.
Light out of darkness. Who would think
from such a place a mind could come back whole
and bring so much?

xxi.

The Sleep of Reason

Half-masochist, I sit here face to face
with images which Goya etches out
of dream and fantasy – grotesqueries
I'd rather do without, which scarify
absurdity and ignorance and worse.

He sinks me deep into a time and place
I don't much care to visit, where the mind
has dropped its guard and reason gone to sleep.
That time is never far away.
Nor will these monstrous forms disperse,

for what they symbolise is commonplace
for satirists of every age and stripe –
the long ears of the credulous,
the unction of the charlatan,
the owlish stare of the perverse.

The pages turn without a hiding-place.
Through eighty plates there is no anodyne
to mitigate the mind's embattlement.
We're at the far end of Enlightenment
where reason slides into reverse.

xxii.

Gauguin's Vision

This painted panel is to be the last
before he goes to die. The fresco moves
from birth to death in darkening episodes
through demi-Edens over which
a grey-faced deity presides.

The golden women in their prime
gaze out through melancholy eyes.
In the late tropic sun they know
that all must fruit and husk and fall and die
as light and pride of life subsides.

D'Où Venons Nous: Que Sommes Nous mark the wall.
Où Allons Nous completes a trinity
of schoolroom-lettered questioning.
The canvas offers no reply at all
beyond the darkening sequence it provides.

Tahiti, Brittany and Arles –
the questions and the silences the same.
No difference except in dialect.
There is no other-world outside the frame.
No gloss is offered. Nothing like a guide.

Vincent's Chair

He's put it down, the pipe, to take his brush
and touch up "Vincent" on the corner chest.
Perched on the rushes of the chair,
they tell you, do the pouch and pipe,
their owner can't be far away.

It's Vincent's own chair waiting patiently
on the tiled floor for him to finish off,
pocket the pipe and take his seat again
once the last strokes are dry. (That won't take long
in Arles' oven of a summer day.)

The *Ding an sich*. A right-of-insight claim
to all rush-bottomed kitchen chairs.
It's unassailable. "Look close,
it's what it is," the painter says,
"and how it means to stay."

Elsewhere, his day may swirl
with sunflowers and cypresses.
But the kitchen chair's content to wait
for the wet paint to dry
and the old pipe to be put away.

xxiv.

Magritte's Mirror

Abracadabra! On the stage,
magicians wave their wands and bring things back.
But not Magritte. With him they disappear
for good into a magic box or stay
suspended in mid-air.

The lady's torso, cut in half,
is not about to be restored.
The man whose mirror fails to show
more than the rear view of his head
will stare for ever at his hair.

Not sleight of hand but sleight of mind.
What is deceived is not the eye alone.
It's the whole space we occupy
which passes into nothingness,
revealing neither who nor where.

Yet everything's meticulous.
Illusion one could almost touch.
A void that's documentary.
Alien, chimeric worlds
painted with fastidious care.

Angel of the North

Eyeless in Gateshead on his pithead mound
the great metal angel stands
deep-rooted in the Tyneside soil, his wings
outspread and aeronautical,
a totem for the land around.

We have particulars from head to foot –
his height, construction and design –
but no clear kite-mark of his kind.
Who, if a guardian, is he meant to guard?
And on what footing does he take his ground?

We recognise a grave acknowledgement
of the long ranks of the mining dead;
and greet him also as a figurehead
of new life springing from the old –
a steel Prometheus Unbound.

And yet that iron mask remains
unyielding and mysterious.
Impassive, faceless, inarticulate.
A mercy awkward to discern.
A benediction gone to ground.

The *David* of Michelangelo

He's sizing up Goliath with disdain,
and any moment now will loose the sling
from his enormous palm.
He's conscious that all eyes are watching him.
But since the living God will guide his arm

he stands unflinching in a kind of
languid resolution, a defiant
nonchalance, awaiting triumphs
which are not in doubt. He knows
he will not come to harm.

Embodiment of classic flesh and bone,
here is a figure from Mount Helicon
as much as David fighting Philistines.
A junior Apollo. With a lyre,
he'd turn out odes instead of writing psalms.

And in that multi-cultured, hybrid form,
emancipated from the matrix-stone,
he stands gigantic, unashamed
in his not-too-Hebrew nakedness,
confronting bluster with Olympian calm.

Ego Hugo

Ego Hugo. Dead a hundred years,
but at St Peter Port you'll find him still
bustling around inside his citadel
among the lustre and display
and bric-à-brac and devotees.

There still his exile's *quartier-général*,
his self-installed meridian,
his island-in-an-island with a grey
distant view of Normandy
across the Channel's chevaux-de-frise.

In silhouette he's in his look-out still,
dashing off *Les Misérables*,
trashing *Napoléon le petit*;
larger than life and making the most of it.
He means to see as the Almighty sees,

and let the whole world know of it,
his eye on history and the main chance.
Great fornicator. Self-created
man of destiny who's made himself
the patron saint of refugees.

xxviii.

Leaves of Grass

My ancient Whitman, badly stitched
and short of backing, fell apart.
In expiation I went out and bought
the first edition of the *Leaves of Grass* –
the very earliest gatherings,

the paean to the common man
out of a Brooklyn Helicon,
uncommon and baroque –
the book which conjured Emerson to praise
"incomparable things"

from one in shirt and dungarees,
a Yankee transcendentalist
in union with the universe,
retailing rhapsodies about
his urges and imaginings.

A prophet-poet on a fugal high.
A psychic fantasist, and yet
an impresario who knew
what nerves to touch, and how to put on show
his appetites and wanderings.

Shamans

Under the rock at Drakensberg,
ochre dancers twine with fish
and herds of running antelope.
Possessed by spirits and familiars,
shamans arch their backs in pain.

Women stamp and clap their hands
to make the eland come.
The shamans fly and elongate.
They swim in water with an eel.
They bleed to bring a healing rain.

After the moon and stars have set,
and the leopard's safe inside his cave,
with ash and earth the bushman paints
totem and fetish on the wall
to make the spirits rise again.

Listen. Below the rock you'll hear
the urgent drum and ritual
of man and spirit-animal
across ten thousand years,
vibrating in the lower brain.

xxx.

Oracle

Delphi brought discovery. Pumpkins
with proud umbilica; capers on stalks;
and the dark cavern underground
where in narcotic ecstasy
the oracle made moans

which could be prophecy
when money talked. Petitioners
wound up the Sacred Way
with cash in hand. I climbed it too,
discarding olive stones

and thinking of the ballyhoo
of Jason with his Argonauts,
who sowed a field with serpents' teeth
which turned into battalions
of battle-ready clones.

Myths swelled like pumpkin here
beside Apollo's holy spring.
Eyes on stalks, the faithful watched
the frenzied priestess as she conjured
riddles out of grunts and groans.

xxxi.

Gods at Madurai

The towering gópurams of Madurai –
ten thousand gods and goddesses
cascading tier upon tier
from the highest sill – are meant
to take your breath away. Such size

and colour and divine event!
Inside, a lotus pool; a pillared hall;
a sacred bull; an elephant;
and priests attendant on the sacred stones
they sweep and dress and solemnize.

Out in the street, the surge and swirl
of auto-rickshaws, hawkers, bicycles,
and all the Tamil tongues at work.
A pungent melting-pot of smells
under the flame of enterprise.

The gods rise up above the fumes
in tier upon tier of pantheon,
blessed and fierce and fecund, yet
their gestures are unchanging.
Unimpressible, those staring eyes.

Pantocrator

High in his conch at Cefalù
the icon-Christ will stare you out.
There's nowhere you can slide away
from the compulsion of his eye,
the figured blessing of his hand.

The Judge-Redeemer of the world
is getting ready to foreclose,
but holds a Gospel with mosaic words
forgiving all their debts to those
who come to understand.

Cunning Byzantium which knew
the interplay of power and art
took care in placing tesserae to show
in brow and eye by whose authority
the vault and cosmos stand.

The Godhead in his golden firmament
demands repentance even though
from the beginning He has known
which characters are set in stone
and which are only traced in sand.

Le Thoronet

At twenty, it took hold of me –
near fields of lavender in Var, a place
where simple masonry conveys
the numinous; a place where narrow shafts of light
deepen shadow on Cistercian stone.

A house where prayer followed, day and night,
an ever-turning liturgy
of collect and of gloria;
the rote of Matins, Lauds and Prime
and Terce and Sext and None.

Agnostic Le Corbusier was moved
to praise the witness of its stones,
their symmetries and plenitude.
Here all's austere and decorous,
a beauty never overblown.

An abbey without gilt or ornament –
its breadth and depth and length and height
devoted to an inwardness
where faith may venture to reach out
beyond reserve to the unknown.

xxxiv.

Candles for the Dead

In Madikeri's quiet church,
the ashram at the valley head,
we lit a candle for the dead
of yesterday and long ago,
turning prayer into flame.

There's no reconnaissance can reach the dead.
We have no bearings on them; no topography.
But when their residue is love,
we hold them in our hearts and seek a way
towards them through the form of flame.

No other thing can pierce the dark
like love's unswayed creative fire.
Primal, vital, conquering light
in the votive candle's spire
turns to spiritual flame.

We long that disembodied souls,
refined into eternity
beyond the reach of human word,
discharged from Earth – may yet be stirred
to know us by a prayer and flame.

Kyoto Garden

The garden-shrine of Ryoan-ji.
A seasonless parterre of sand
raked into enigmatic whorls
around the shores of island-stones,
fastidious and monochrome.

Nothing here but by design –
the seeming motion of the sand
and seeming rise of island-stone
invite the eye to move
from rock to swirling comb

and back, and back again until it finds
a point of equilibrium,
a harbourage of calm.
Around the whiteness of the sand
a wall of ancient loam

holds its possession tight and tells
that nothing good comes without sanctuary,
that it's the frame that frees the space within,
that even flawless images require
a shelter and a home.

xxxvi.

Mandala of Sand

Exotic in the beaux-arts gallery,
Tibetan monks in saffron and maroon
are working on a mandala of sand.
A crowd in checks and denim gathers round,
inquisitive but quite indifferent

that all the colours and precise design
are predetermined, with the fine grains tapped
just so, to make a testament –
a kind of blueprint for the mind;
a mental road-map to enlightenment.

Around the mandala is traced
a triple cordon, guarding the disk within,
holding the icon tight, lending the inward eye
a focus and capacity to see
the way to disembodiment.

But all is mutable. The monks will take
the finished mandala, and pray,
and pass the image down into a stream
till all is washed away, its power
invisible and immanent.

xxxvii.

Moore: *Reclining Figure*

Distinct and indistinct.
The torso tells of hill and bone,
of lap and cavity,
of shoulder and of slope.
Clouds are passing over the thigh.

Look closer and a mollusc shell
is bedded in the jut of knee.
Winds caress the arms and spine.
The face withdraws into itself,
leaving a weathered eye.

Form has grown out from stone.
Seas have worn its angularities
into a pebble nakedness.
Pass it on a tidal sand
and you might well walk by.

But outcropped on the moor it seems
a block eroded by the wind,
a dark rock in an open place,
and in its likeness to a human shape,
a curiosity.

xxxviii.

Silence at Briggflatts

Turn down the unassuming country lane
to where a roof of Pennine stone
is facing off the wind and rain.
This is the quiet house, the place
where silent Quakers come to meet.

Step out of dank and drizzle. Lift the latch
on four-square stillness.
Faint and grey, the morning light
slides round sill and mullion
as if its purpose was retreat.

Under the shadow of the fell
where Fox stood up and planted deep
the word of God in local hearts,
this place was built to garner in
stores of spiritual wheat.

A place to guard the inward light
and power of communion
which needs no liturgy or bell.
For these insiders, means of grace
ripened in the soul's own heat.

Pen-y-Ghent

So to the nab of Pen-y-Ghent
where moor's impounded in a maze of walls
and landscape speaks in accents that I know –
a tongue of scars and rakes and becks
straight from the Norse. A land of spur and knoll,

rough pasture on the valley side,
a cold wind scouring over scarp
from Ribblehead. Here is my own;
my latitude and dialect,
my discourse and parole.

From this bleak Sinai the moors roll out
austere and puritan and fall
in tussock, stone and reed
sodden to the valley floors
down gill and swallow-hole.

If there's illusion here,
it's deeply rooted in the bone
and ineradicable.
This is native heath and home,
meridian and pole.

The Automatic Self

i.

The Automatic Self

I think of the workings of my heart and viscera,
  and all the organs of my automatic self –

the sprouting of nail and hair; the enterprise
  of enzyme and bacteria;

the circus-factory of the living cell
  with its strange machinery;

the oddities at work there –
  organelles (half-cage, half-crucible)

and, with helical whip, the ringmaster DNA
  putting the whole performance through its paces.

Who is the owner
  of this shifting stage?

Sinew, nerve and vessel, it was not I
  who assembled them.

All of my processes are spontaneous:
  the pipes gurgling away.

Even the routes of thought are hidden from me:
  the putting of things together.

I have no option but to take delivery,
  and make the best I can of it.

ii.

Another Man

At birth I took delivery of hypothalamus
and double hemispheres compressed
into a tenement of endless stairs
and corridors and wires and cellarage,
only to find my quarters bare,
unfurnished, second-best,
and with another man in charge
of all my flows and processes.

It's odd, this habitat where I'm confined
with a doppelganger self, control declined
to me, the putative lessee –
the key to all my functioning assigned
to a master-switcher that I cannot see
who has the use of more than half my mind.

iii.

Heart and Mind

Govern my own heart? Not a bit.
I cannot set its metronome;
its constant systole-diastole,
its filling and depletion.

The lung, too, is out of my control.
It will not tolerate,
against its mastery of rise and fall,
an alien intervention.

My spleen and pancreas obey
precise instructions. None are mine.
Bone, flesh and skin are not within
my sphere of operation.

Yet in the mind I play some kind of part
and seek a proof right here,
down on the page,
in this narration.

iv.

Wound

Of body all I see is boundary –
mirrored face, veneer of skin.
Under the epidermis, tendon and vein
fork out and fade away.

A wound brings things to light;
puts raw flesh on display,
bares fibre and capillary,
the red blood flowing out.

This is the time to see
how body's forces rally round,
how its auxiliaries defend
its order and integrity.

Nothing will be left to chance.
The only part I have to play
is bear the pain and walk away
and leave things to their own defence.

v.

Suppleness

I think of motors
of the body's suppleness
that yield and flex,
contract and magnify –

articulations of the neck and limb,
the spine's plasticity,
and what is fluid and resilient
in hand and eye.

Also the mouth's softness;
flicker of tongue;
pliancy of lip
and cheek;

and tenderness of touch,
the skin's mobility,
as I chance my arm,
and speak.

Night Watch

i.

Night Watch

On the bridge of sleep
I come to the night watch
and take my place.
It's here I must remain
till my turn is over.

The darkness of dream
engulfs me; outlook
grows obscure as all
horizons fade and
merge into fantasy.

Ships pass unlit,
unsignalling, their names
nul or illegible.
From distant waters
comes a sound of guns.

No captain's to be found.
If there are orders,
no one has thought fit
to post them, or display
a destination.

Sometimes I pick out
shapes of passengers
along a far deck,
looking towards me,
still and familiar.

They do not try
to speak, but stay
always in shadow,
impassive, rigid
and expressionless.

They do not ask
if we're on course, on time.
No hands are cupped
against the faint wind
to light a cigarette.

What moves the vessel on?
Beneath my feet
I seem to feel
a seaway and a tide
under the heave and swell,

but never can bring home
its sense and direction.
There is no compass, and
for reef or strait
there is no pilot.

No measure's made
of distance, and for depth
there are no soundings.
No wished-for harbour
is ever reached.

The ship's cargoes
have no manifest.
Whatever episodes
unfold, there'll be no log,
or any narrative.

In the small hours shimmer
Arctic aurora
and St Elmo's fire.
Outlandish happenings
are commonplace.

Hatches open. Lumber
of all kinds is heaved up
from the hold and loaded
into the lifeboats –
books and violins.

Out of fog emerge
ominous warnings
of storm and shipwreck.
Suddenly the deck
is full of admirals

with braid and medals,
flagging orders,
waving telescopes.
The wheel is spinning
and the canvas flaps.

A kind of hornpipe
is developing.
The crew dance faster
and faster till there's
no one standing.

Bells have rung over and over.
My watch is ending.
The passengers have gone
below. Strands of light
mark the horizon.

As the ship fades, I try
to hold in memory
the dancing faces
but fail, utterly,
to bring them ashore.

What declaration
can I make? The dream
is coded, and will prove,
come morning,
hard to break.

Only at length
shall I determine
what of the watch
was pantomime, and what
to take as warning.

ii.

The Unreal Estate

Night, and once more I enter
the unreal estate,
the unmarked avenues,
the nameless quarters,

the journey full of sudden flight,
of shifting sequences,
of strange connections,
of action constantly distorted.

These fractured episodes –
they're more than glints of memory
in sleep's darkness. But by what means
have I arrived at such a pitch?

Surely the quarry
can answer for the chase?
And who but I can identify
the trackers who pursue, and why?

Yet all remains disguised.
There's no way here to pin down time and place –
no border where you get to see
proofs of identity.

Nor any warning of the point
where you may come upon a way
which seems your own but where
the road is closed and overgrown.

iii.

Night Flight

I draw the blinds and wait for sleep
to draw its own blinds down
on form and congruence –
to shutter and escape
the concrete and tangible.

All is unscheduled now; all place
and time unspecified.
I enter the shadows of the terminal
where dreamers face
flights of anxiety.

Is this reality or masquerade?
Am I the pilot
or a nervous passenger
bent on getting away – afraid of freefall –
seeking a soft landing?

Here come dream-companions –
wildly mismatched, but
acting with complicity.
I hear opinions
which are sordid and banal.

Things become ominous.
The dreamer's rattled by
urgent wake-up calls.
Is he (am I?) nearing the terminus
of this journey?

Can he or I attain a gate
where, before waking, we might
catch a final flight
to a non-hostile state,
a safe conclusion?

iv.

Peculiar Readings

Awake, I have quartz and mercury
as close companions.
They are precise
and calibrate my coming and going
almost to perfection.

Asleep it's otherwise –
all dials out of sync
with peculiar readings
which I can't make out
and, waking, forget.

V.

Time and Again

Time and again I find myself in plays
which have no character or plot
worthy of précis, let alone praise.
Well-crafted drama they are not.

Mine are always leading roles
in these enactments – not by choice
nor as director who controls
the action, or has any voice.

No performance ever reaches
a conclusion. Yet the plays go on and on
with the same outlandish features
in the same benighted auditorium.

Worlds Apart

i.

Open the Atlas

Open the atlas. Here the world is calm
and clear and amenable,
the continents all lined up to appear
on the same apron stage;
the globe massaged
into a planisphere.

The map lies docile on the page,
all frontiers fixed, the oceans still.
No earthquakes or eclipse.
Hot desert, forest, ice,
fjord and Everest
all soft under the fingertips.

For sure the frontiers will not hold.
Time will bleach out
imperial colours.
Catastrophe will sap all
contours, kings, caudillos,
ayatollahs.

Yet for a moment taste
the quiet of illusion,
the continents at rest,
entirely still,
ocean becalmed,
the nations motionless.

ii.

Mappa Mundi

A cloister template.
Lands of Ham and Shem
patched up from Genesis
and Prester John.

A map of travellers' tales
and Holy Writ;
Gog and Magog,
Rome and Ararat

all packed within
Creation's womb.
At the world's navel
sits Jerusalem.

Monks know cell and scroll
better than high seas;
seek illumination
in apocalypse.

Scholastic geography,
plying minster roads,
would never get you
to your journey's end.

iii.

Golden Age

A sheet from the *Theatrum* of the world,
Andalucia in the Golden Age.
The impresario-cartographer
knows how to set the stage –
the province dovetailed with the sea
and hemmed in tight with bishoprics –

the Silver Highway northward to Madrid
funnelling New World bullion –
ports where puny caravels
sail westwards after gold and spice –
bulging sierras, cordilleras crowned
with molehill villages –

and across all the snow-fed Guadalquivir –
gran rey de Andalucía –
washing the walls of Cordoba,
a hundred miles of shallows to Seville,
debouching through the duneland and salinas
(*vulgo La Maresma*) to the sea.

Seville imperial – at its apogee
in 1579 – the town secure –
sugar and silver in the port –
King Philip proud in his Escorial.
Eight years ago Lepanto smashed the Turk.
Nine, before the Armada. On the cusp.

A cliché of the theatre of Spain,
with one wing leading to the open sea,
the other drawing inward to Castille –
all fixed with history's collodion.
Within the bay of Cadiz, galleons fight.
On the ocean, wide-mouthed monsters lie in wait.

iv.

Surrealist World

A map with an equator like a snake
sliding between distorted continents
towards the South Pacific where
huge Easter Island rears up like a bear.

A psychedelic geography.
A manifesto-map which does not show
the way you want to go
but tells you where to stand.

Iles Marquises; Archipel Bismarck;
all of them *térritoires primitives*
where primal psyche's held to breathe
the air of uncorrupted myth.

The South Seas swell. Zero meridian
skewers a fattened Papua.
We're in strange waters here; are meant to learn
new scales and latitudes.

Northward, a massive Russia looms
where fetish yields to commissar.
Westward, the USA's squashed flat
by Mexico and Labrador.

In Europe, nothing's left to see
except a Greater Germany.
In 1929, no city stands
except – a pimple on the Hun – *Paris.*

V.

Peters' Projection

Pin up the Peters map. All swollen, gold
and post-colonial, the pear
of Africa holds centre stage.
Stage right, immaculate in Lincoln green
comes parsnip South America,
proportionately lean.

"All's fair and square," the map says; "all
my ratios are justified."
Yet something's odd. You look above
fifty degrees of latitude,
and lands are squashed out like a tube.
Iceland's turned into a squid.

Mercator took the greatest pains
but no way could he hope to stretch
tropic to pole with the same pull
or tune his parallels to perfect pitch.
And nothing's changed. The fact is that
the globe just will not lie down flat.

Haikus for a Summer Day

Deep black on shorn fields,
litters, plump, of new-baled hay.
Sun glints on their skin.

At noon, a great roar.
Fighters spattering upland
with terrified sheep.

Down swoops a blackbird,
alarmed – its paratrooper
voice fires off abuse.

A low scud and zip –
some wren in the undergrowth
heading for cover.

* * *

At the river-fall,
boys loll in shade where willows
furrow the water.

Daylight is fading.
Edge of shadow unhouses
sun from the treetops.

Swifts wheel and sabre,
cutting the clouds to ribbons
of silver and grey.

Dusk brings out chafers.
Deep-throated tractors harvest
by headlight and moon.

Haikus for a Winter Day

Out on the fen, ice –
frost lining fields and ditches;
feathering sluices.

Shrouded, the river;
muffled, the rhythm of oars.
Ghost willows hover.

Sun's wafer rises.
Frozen, the sky receives it
with colourless palm.

Rowers' hands slacken.
Boat drifts on stagnant water
in silence of mist.

Homeward, cold-marrowed;
light failing; ice underfoot;
breath raw in the lungs.

Objects are fading.
Fog shrouds levels and willow;
gathers the river.

Lighting of windows.
Sulphurous coal-smoke mingles
with thickening mist.

Over the dark fen,
out of the sharpening air,
a far train rumbles.

Winter Day Above Dent

High in this circle of familiar hills,
mind fuses with their stretch and rising,
moulds to their wrap and folding,
and the sweep of scar and ghyll;

and down where Helm's Knott swells,
stubbled with heather, latches on
to the great Fault splitting Lakes from Dales,
where Pennines butt up against lakeland fell.

All unity, the valley's scoop appears
from this vantage-point, but underground
the strata are at odds: one step and you're out
by a hundred million years.

Swift becks lay bare the skeleton;
disclose the fractures and the shattered bones
of breccia and conglomerate –
the twist and grind and shudder of convulsion.

But in the dale, a daub of green and brown
covers the sync- and anti-cline.
Its soft contours mantle the rend and fission
which aeons of wind and rain have whittled down.

Now all is calm. The fossil shells
and coral colonies lie silent
under upland farms. Deep seams of limestone
bed down quietly with shale.

Sedge glows in the setting winter sun
like fox's fur: long capes of shadow fall
from drystone walls: ice underfoot
warns that the short bright day will soon be done.

Intrusion

High up the scarp, just
under the lid of cloud,
a pair of humdrum
railway carriages
are puttering smugly
past the flanks of Whernside
and of Pen-y-Ghent.

Rail has long had moorland's
measure, laying down laws
of tilt and gradient,
slicing through shaw and fell,
piercing pike and crag,
striding valley heads
on viaduct stilts.

Roads are milder – turn
and dip and tolerate
moor's encroachment.
When the right time comes,
the land won't hesitate
to take them back, quilt them
with reed and sphagnum.

But rail is bedded in
and with a deeper brand;
pick and dynamite have
scarred and cauterised.
Its track – even when green,
with the steel long gone –
will last like Pyramids.

Riddle

It is an anvil ringing
with blow after blow.

It is bellows and coal
and the grip of tongs.

It is a diadem of steel
with torque and clasp.

It is the raw pith of a tree
stripped of its bark.

It is seen in an eye
which abhors light.

It is heard in the stab
of clocks in quiet rooms.

It is the teeth of a trap
clenched on bone.

It is an unhealed wound
to be borne alone.